LOSS OF A MARRIAGE

IN THIS VERY HOUR

Devotions for Your Time of Need

LOSS OF A MARRIAGE

IN THIS VERY HOUR

Devotions for Your Time of Need

B. J. FUNK

BROADMAN
& HOLMAN
PUBLISHERS

Nashville, Tennessee

© 1994
by Broadman & Holman Publishers
All rights reserved

Printed in the United States of America

4253-79
0-8054-5379-2

Dewey Decimal Classification: 242.4
Subject Heading:
DEVOTIONAL LITERATURE // DIVORCE
Library of Congress Card Catalog Number: 94-10748

Unless otherwise indicated, all Scripture references are from the *New King James Version*, copyright © 1979, 1980, 1982, Thomas Nelson, Inc., Publishers. Verses marked (AMP) are from *The Amplified Bible*, Old Testament © 1962, 1964 by Zondervan Publishing House, used by permission; and New Testament © The Lockman Foundation 1954, 1958, 1987, used by permission.

Library of Congress Cataloging-in-Publication Data
Funk, B. J., 1943–
  Devotions for your time of need. Loss of a marriage / by B. J. Funk
   p. cm. — (In this very hour)
  ISBN 0-8054-5379-2
  1. Divorced people—Prayer-books and devotions.
2. Divorce—Religious aspects—Christianity—Prayer-books and devotions—English. 3. Bereavement—Religious aspects—Christianity—Prayer-books and devotions. I. Title. II. Series.
BV4596.D58F86   1994
242'.646—dc20   94-10748
                                                                              CIP

*To each member of my divorce support groups.
You're living proof that divorce
is not a terminal illness.*

Contents

Prologue: Healing a Scar 1
1. God's Guidance 6
2. A Remedy for Loneliness 7
3. Rejection 8
4. Leave Your Worries with Him 9
5. What to Do with Fear 10
6. Finding Peace in the Midst of Pain 11
7. God Will Help 12
8. Somedays I Think I Can 13
9. The Gift of Tears 14
10. Who Can Heal a Broken Heart? 15
11. Find Your Focus 16
12. Knocking Down the Idol 17
13. A Thankful Heart—Even in Divorce? .. 18
14. Casting Stones 20
15. What About the Children? 21
16. Facing Failure 22
17. If Only I Had… 23

18. Victims 24
19. Who Won Anyway 25
20. Can't We Just Skip Forgiveness? 26
21. God Is Listening 28
22. One Woman's Turning Point 29
23. Letting Go 30
24. Take Time to Heal 31
25. A Different Love 32
26. What's Wrong with Me? 33
27. Searching for Hope 34
28. Grieving 35
29. Can I Ever Trust Again? 36
30. Is God Mad at Me? 37
31. Becoming Real 38
Epilogue: Moving on with Life 40

PROLOGUE

Healing a Scar

I have a scar that's healing. Perhaps you have it too. It's a scar called divorce; and even though my scar is not red and puffy now, I know it's there. But it doesn't hurt as much as it used to.

I'm learning to live with my scar. I hope you are too. I'm learning that I can take it with me to the movies, the grocery store, even to church and it's not nearly as noticeable as it was. Sometimes others are surprised to discover I have this scar.

At first, the cut was so deep, the wound so penetrating, that my whole body ached and ached. That went on for months. Then I found I could move one limb, then another, then another; and the more I ventured out, the better I got. Parts of me that had decided to die because of the scar gradually started to move again. My mouth was the last part to heal. Gradually, I was able to form a smile, and eventually even laughter.

Now, years later, when I walk down the street or get in the middle of a crowd, I almost forget about that scar. But at the beginning you never could have convinced me that would happen!

And what was the beginning for me? The beginning was the ending of a marriage I just knew could never die. After all, weren't we the perfect couple? In our college days, he was the dream guy of my sorority, and I was the sweetheart of his fraternity. Life moved at an exhilarating pace, always accompanied by his marvelous humor and his ability to make me laugh. We never argued. Life was fun, fun, fun!

After our marriage, we lived almost ten wonderful years on that laughter and in peaceful harmony. He received a master of divinity degree and later went back for another degree in the medical field. Two precious sons completed our joy. As his success began to show financial results, we bought our first home. Always generous, he provided well for the boys and me. Family dinners out were frequent. He was very attentive, calling daily from work just to make sure I was okay. I was completely content. How could life get any sweeter?

I had noticed, however, somewhere around the tenth year, that he was gone a lot. He kept long hours now—all of it, I told myself, for the boys and me. I noticed, too, that bottles of alcohol now rested in our kitchen cabinet and that many nights after work, he drank and went to sleep watching television. I pleaded. He seemed not to notice. Most of all, I realized the laughter had faded.

When I speak now at singles' gatherings, I sometimes say, "I should have won the Miss Vulnerability or Miss Gullible award during those days." I was completely trusting and unsuspecting that the man I had married—until death was to part us—was living a double life and was ready to leave me. The night he told me was a nightmare. He tried to soak the cruel words in tenderness, but all I could do was hold my stomach and walk from room to room in our dark house, crying until dawn entered the den window. Never has a night, before or since, been as painful or as bleak. I had never known such hopelessness.

Then miraculously, but apparently with considerable confusion, he decided to let go of his other life. He wanted to know if he could stay. How dare he place this tremendous burden on me? He had handed me the cruelest pain I could imagine, and now he wanted to start over? Just like that? I had to decide if our marriage was worth fighting for. Yet, I knew in my heart that love isn't something I turn on and off, like the faucet at my sink. I still loved him very much, and we had two sons who were counting on us.

I decided our marriage was worth too much for us to give up on it so quickly. We would start over. However, I cautiously eyed each day, and suspicion was my constant companion. I shared my pain with only a few close friends. I determined that no one else was to know. Certainly not the many friends we enjoyed in the dynamic church we had joined. Certainly not my neighbors. Certainly not my parents or my sister and her family.

So I kept smiling, losing fifteen pounds in a couple of weeks, and wondering each day how I could ever trust my husband again. I worked at trusting for five years. He worked hard at it too, showering me with gifts and attention. More family dinners out. More family vacations. More fun. Our wonderful laughter even returned.

But at the end of five years, I saw a familiar pattern emerging—long hours, more drinking, less communication, and a general restlessness. The dark night of five years earlier had returned, but this time there was no indication from him that he wanted to try again. One day he slipped out into the night and into his anticipated new life as a single man. I went to bed for days, and soon the hideous word *divorce* had become an indellible part of my life.

I could say, "That's when Jesus walked in," but that wouldn't be right. He had walked in five years earlier—in that first season of pain—holding my hand and helping me through the insecurities and rejection. He held my hand now as my husband walked out the door, and He gave me a steady source of strength. I don't know how anyone gets through divorce without Jesus. I really don't. The pain is too great. The uncertainties too real. The nights too long.

The tears too deep. We can make it only as we realize that in our weakness He is our strength. Laughter did finally come back to my life. But it wasn't because of any man. It was because of Jesus.

I wish we could completely eliminate the scar called divorce. But as long as we are living inside imperfect bodies, carrying around our tempers, our carnal desires, our selfish responses, some men and women who marry will not be compatible. Many couples are fortunate enough to move past the incompatibilities and onto mature growth in marriage. But for those who find themselves victims of one of life's biggest heartaches, I prayerfully hope this book offers encouragement and comfort.

1

God's Guidance

You will guide me with your counsel, and afterward receive me to glory.
Psalm 73:24

In all your ways acknowledge Him, and He shall direct your paths.
Proverbs 3:6

You are faced with many decisions. Never before have so many thoughts and questions been hurled at you. Well-meaning friends and relatives who don't want you to suffer often seek to console by unwittingly pointing you in the wrong direction.

If you want to handle your divorce as a Christian, it is imperative that you seek godly counsel. Find a praying Christian friend, confide in him or her, and then watch God work. You will be amazed at the newfound power of prayer, amazed that God had your answers worked out before you even asked Him.

Our best counselor is the Holy Spirit. As you learn to turn your burdens over to Him, you will learn to hear His voice. If you are in doubt about any decision you have to make, wait until you receive His counsel. Divine guidance will come through prayer, through Bible reading, through circumstances, or through the words of a friend. In my dining room, a plaque hangs that reads, "God always gives the best to those who leave the choice to Him." Tell God that you want His best for you, and that you are willing to wait until He shows you His choice in your decisions.

2

A Remedy for Loneliness

Fear not, for I am with you . . . I will strengthen you, yes, I will help you.
Isaiah 41:10

There will be times when you will be very lonely. The house will be quiet, your friends will all be at home with their families, and you will be by yourself.

For me, one of the loneliest times was my first New Year's Eve without my husband. My two young sons were outside shooting rockets with neighbors as the clock ticked away the old year. I sat on the sofa by myself and watched the happy faces on the TV screen. People were hugging and laughing as a new year began. Suddenly an empty darkness began to envelope me. A new 365 days seemed like more than I could bear. An indescribable sense of loneliness filled my heart over me.

God reminds us that He is with us, He will strengthen us, and He will help us. The great miracle of these words is that they are absolutely true. Sitting still in the darkness that New Year's Eve, I realized that

God was my best and closest friend. He would never leave me.

Loneliness doesn't have to smother us. We can be alone and yet not be by ourselves. God wants to prove to you that He can provide a steady friendship, one that will take you through the dark hours of your day.

3

REJECTION

> I will be a Father to you, and you shall be my sons and daughters, says the Lord Almighty.
> *2 Corinthians 6:18*

The biggest hurdle I had to cross during divorce was rejection. I convinced myself that I must be terribly ugly or my husband would have stayed with me. There had to be a reason he left. Maybe it was that crooked tooth, or perhaps I was too tall.

During those first few weeks after the initial shock, I felt all men were my enemy. If the man I had lived with for fifteen years didn't want me, I assumed no one else ever would.

But I was wrong. Wrong to place a prison of rejection around myself because of the actions of one person. Wrong to let my self-worth fall because of one person's response.

Slowly my wounded ego began to heal as I climbed out of my narrow view. I realized that there were many, many good people in the world and that many of them could love me.

How did that new understanding emerge? Slowly—as I began to see God's love as a basic need in my life. I envisioned Him wrapping His arms around me daily. With His love reaching out to me, I began to see myself anew. I am loveable. I am important. I am of infinite value.

Resting in His tender care, your damaged self-esteem can heal. Whenever you begin to think you have little worth, repeat the above Bible verse to yourself. Your heavenly Father thinks you're worth a lot. A holy God calls you His son or daughter. That should make anyone walk a little taller.

4

LEAVE YOUR WORRIES WITH HIM

Be anxious for nothing, but in everything by prayer and supplication, with thanksgiving, let your requests be made known to God.

Philippians 4:6

How comforting it is to know that our God wants us to ask for His help. He wants us to leave our petitions with Him. You'd think He had enough to do without our worries! However, this verse tells us that He desires to know our concerns. He is pleased when we bring our anxious moments before His throne. And unlike earthly friends, He has all the time in the world to listen to your needs.

Separation and divorce will bring plenty of anxious moments. But you don't have to spend all your time and energy fretting. You have a choice. You may choose to share your worries with a Friend—a best Friend. God desires that you tell Him how you feel.

Spend time with Him. Tell Him everything. Don't be concerned that His ears will find your petitions unbelievable, that His purity cannot bear your sins. Because of Jesus, you and I have access to God's heart. Because of Jesus, the stain of divorce has already been conquered on the cross. Because of Jesus, you and I have hope that our brokenness can be turned into something of beauty.

Go ahead. Tell it to Jesus. You'll be amazed at the relief you feel each time you do.

5

What to Do with Fear?

> So we may boldly say, "The Lord is my helper; I will not fear. What can man do to me?"
> *Hebrews 13:6*

Fear loves to visit a newly separated or divorced person. Fear likes to intimidate. Its job is to make your life as difficult as possible. Fear wants you to believe an end to your present pain will never come.

Fear likes to come into our lives in many ways. Divorce seeks to rob us of our strength. Fear marches in, reminding us that we used to be married to someone who can still cause problems for us. Fear tells us that divorce doesn't end the day the papers are signed, that divorce goes on and on.

This Bible verse tells us that we can claim God's help. How does it say to claim His help? Not timidly, but boldly. We can confidently ask for His help, knowing for sure that He is more powerful than any fear we can have.

Pray this prayer daily: "Father God, I ask for your help through the difficulties of this day. I cannot do it alone. I am powerless against the fears in my life. But You are my victory. I place my fears before You, confident that only You can give me strength."

6

FINDING PEACE IN THE MIDST OF PAIN

Peace I leave with you, my peace I give to you; not as the world gives do I give to you. Let not your heart be troubled, neither let it be afraid.

John 14:27

The world has no peace to give. You're up early in the morning, dashing around the kitchen and running through the house on your way to a job filled with the world's problems. After work, you hurry to the grocery store and then to the post office to collect this day's bills. The rest of the day is filled with errands and responsibilities. Where is this peace the Bible speaks of? And how can you find a portion of it?

Jesus is our peace. He has left peace for you and me. It is a gift. It is, as Philippians 4:7 tells us, a peace that passes all earthly understanding.

Once I have received the Prince of Peace into my heart, the only way I can lose my peace is by my choice. Peace remains with me unless I allow trouble and fear to enter my heart.

Sound difficult? It is, especially if you're doing all the work. Divorced people are notorious for thinking there is no way out but to worry and plan, plan and worry until this hideous battle is all over.

But there is a better way. Ask Jesus to fill your days with His peace. Then prayerfully lay today's worries at the foot of His cross.

Take comfort in these words: "Now may the Lord of peace Himself give you peace always in every way. The Lord be with you all" (2 Thess. 3:16).

7

God Will Help

Fear not . . . be not dismayed . . . I will strengthen you, Yes, I will help you, I will uphold you with My righteous right hand.

Isaiah 41:10

These words of Isaiah fell limply into my heart. How could I possibly "fear not"? My husband of fifteen years had left, I had two young sons depending on me to hold what was left of our home together, and all the teaching positions I sought were filled.

The phone rang in late September. The principal wanted to see me. An overcrowded classroom would be divided, creating a need for a new teacher. Was I interested? You bet!

Quickly the words of Isaiah jumped off the page and did cartwheels on my unbelief, landing specifically on "I will help you." The Scripture came to life before my eyes. What specific burden do you need help with today? Isaiah's words are a message of encouragement, straight from God's heart to yours.

8

SOMEDAYS I THINK I CAN

> He gives power to the faint and weary, and to him who has no might, He increases strength.
> *Isaiah 40:29, AMP*

When my divorce came—during those first days of new grief—my thoughts were often like this:

Somedays I think I can—make it, that is. I awake with a new feeling of resolve. Or perhaps a friend has invited me to dinner; I have something to look forward to!

Then a flashback happens. At the grocery store I see a man who resembles my ex-husband. Fresh pain moves to my heart, and tears burn my eyes.

I never took a college class entitled Broken Marriages 101. I'm having to take this course one day at a time, one hour at a time, on my own. Everything's still so new to me. On most days I'm a good *D* minus. But somedays I think maybe I'm heading for an *A*.

You, too, may experience flashbacks. But God promises to increase your strength. Without His promise of strength you may feel you won't make it; but with Him you have the power to move on.

9

The Gift of Tears

Weeping may endure for a night, but joy comes in the morning.

Psalm 30:5

Can we really trust this verse? Is this simply a comforting thought written by a psalmist with a flair for words? Or can we count on this verse as fact? Will joy ever come?

Weeping doesn't accurately describe the way I cried. I would probably write, "Bawling, desperate sobs and swollen eyes may endure for months . . ."

I never knew I could cry so much. I never knew that the tears started way down in the middle of my stomach and worked their way up to my throat, coming out in loud chokes.

Crying is normal. It's actually a gift. It's the gift of releasing inner hurts so that inner healing can eventually come. The psalmist promises us that after the tears there will be joy.

I'm glad I cried. I'm glad I got it all out so the sunshine of morning's joy could finally warm my heart.

Give yourself permission to accept the gift. And one day, instead of fresh tears, there really will be fresh joy.

10

Who Can Heal a Broken Heart?

He heals the broken hearted and binds up their wounds.

Psalm 147:3

When a person has a physical wound, he or she takes off from work, sees the doctor, and goes to bed. When a person has a divorce wound, he or she can't take off from work and go to bed. Divorce wounds have to be healed while we work and clean house, tuck the children in bed, and empty the garbage. There is no medicine for divorce, and there is no choice but to keep on going while we heal.

Divorced people turn out to be some of the strongest people in the world. That's because they can't stop and nurse their wounds. They don't have time for a pity party. They know that if they are going to survive, they must keep working at it. They must daily depend on God to heal their broken hearts.

I wrote the above verse on index cards and taped it by my phone, on the bathroom medicine cabinet, and on the kitchen wall.

Only God can heal divorce wounds. He's had a lot of practice at it and many, many success stories. Your broken heart is safe in His strong hands.

11

Find Your Focus

> For we have no power against this great multitude that is coming against us; nor do we know what to do, but our eyes are upon You.
> *2 Chronicles 20:12*

Every separated or divorced person has to dig in and prepare to face a great and powerful army that is marching against them. The battle may be from lawyers, relatives, friends, children, or ex-mates. Fear, anxieties, and money problems cause mountains to rise against us. Pain multiplies itself as truth is twisted, as this verse states, and new hurts arise almost daily. Where can we turn for relief?

While we don't have all the answers, we do know where our focus must be. Our eyes must be on Jesus.

While it doesn't mean that our problems will instantly leave or that tomorrow's dawn will bring an end to all the hurt. It clearly means that answers won't come unless our focus is clear.

Take time for prayer. Take time for Bible reading. Tell Jesus that you trust Him to provide the answers you need to rebuild your life.

Then, commit to patiently wait upon Him. He is faithful. Your problems will come to an end one day. There is a new and glorious day ahead. Focus on the Lord. Otherwise, as this Scripture says, you have no might to stand against the pain that would invade your life today.

12

Knocking Down the Idol

> And you shall love the Lord your God with all your heart, with all your soul, with all your mind, and with all your strength. This is the first commandment.
>
> *Mark 12:30*

I really thought I did. Love the Lord with all of me, that is. However, when I first realized there were problems in my marriage, I began to realize that I didn't love God with all of my heart. I loved my husband with all of my heart, and relegated God to second place.

My husband, his needs, and my devoted love to him came first in my life. I suppose my children were next in importance.

God was placed neatly into position number three—I had other gods before Him. I was startled to realize that a church-going Christian such as myself actually didn't obey the first commandment!

God mercifully helped me get my priorities in order. Unfortunately, my husband had to drop completely off his pedestal so that God could climb into His rightful spot. Watching an idol fall is a lesson in humility. First, I had to realize I had a human idol. Then, I had to accept that no other human idol could ever be first place in my life again.

Human beings fail us. We fail others. It's the normal way of humanity. But God never fails. Through Bible reading, prayer, and daily devotions, I was able to give God his rightful spot in my life.

I've never been happier.

13

A Thankful Heart—Even in Divorce?

Thank God in everything—no matter what the circumstances may be, be thankful and give thanks; for this is the will of God for you in Christ Jesus.

1 Thessalonians 5:18, AMP

One thing's for sure. As Christians, we can't pick the Scriptures we want to believe and disregard the rest. If we could, I would have discarded this one long ago.

This verse represents a great personal struggle in my life. But through prayer and through studying the convictions of those who have gone before me in this Christian life, I finally came to realize how much I needed to let this verse be a part of my life—even in divorce.

God does not tell me that I must bite my tongue and thank Him that my husband left my two young sons and me. He does not say that I must send up loud hallelujahs because my dream was shattered and my heart was broken.

He does, however, want me to have an attitude of thanksgiving. Daily I am to offer to Him a thankful heart that sees beyond my present misery and into what will be if I practice gratitude. I am to trust God with this divorce. I am to trust God with all the pain, setbacks, and hurts thrust on my children and me.

If God could work through the evil that placed our Lord on a cross to die, bringing resurrection and triumph from the grave, then I can trust Him to work through the evil of divorce.

I can thank Him that He has a plan worked out—even if it's one I cannot see. I can thank Him that the muddy circumstances of divorce are not too dark for Him to conquer. I can thank Him that He is in control and that there is life after divorce.

14

CASTING STONES

Let him who is without sin among you be the first to throw a stone at her.

John 8:7, AMP

I couldn't believe the words I was hearing. I was on my knees, pouring out my complaints before the Lord, grieving late into the night over the man who had betrayed my trust. Totally unaware that there were any rights but mine, I was a good candidate for the attitude of the Pharisees. Self-righteousness was permitted by righteous blame, or so I thought.

But God decided to deal with it. Right then and there, He whispered, "You're a pilgrim, too." The words cut across my heart as I sat up and looked around the dark room. I saw no one; yet the silent words had been so loud. They fell gently and unaccusingly into my blaming heart.

Suddenly, I had no more words about "my ex-husband's sin." God quietly and lovingly reminded me that I, too, had a long way to go.

Those four words humbled me, taking my focus off continual blame and placing it where it belonged—on my life, my need for the Savior, my growth in the Spirit.

God would handle my former mate. With God's help, I would now continue my own pilgrimage.

15

WHAT ABOUT THE CHILDREN?

But Jesus said, "Let the little children come to Me, and do not forbid them: for of such is the kingdom of heaven."

Matthew 19:14

Other than that awful night when I first learned how my husband viewed our marriage, one other horrid moment of pain stands out. That's when I had to tell our two sons, ages ten and nine, that their daddy would be moving away. Will the horror and shock in their young faces ever leave my memory?

We are a nation doing a great disservice to our children and youth. We've ripped away their trust, torn apart their hearts, and left them to grow up with a suitcase in their hands, moving from weeks to weekends at two different homes. We've allowed them to hear our bitterness, caused them to try to take sides, and often completely abandoned them while searching for our own identity.

It's been fourteen years since my divorce and my heart has never stopped hurting for my children. But I've learned something. I've learned that there is no better place to put our children than right in Jesus' lap. He said, "Bring them to me," and divorced people must learn to do this on a daily basis. His loving arms are the only safe place for children of divorce.

Do something for your children. Show them *you* are going to Jesus, too—that you depend on His help.

Even though you hurt for them, you can trust His care. Your children will eventually get through this crisis if they have your prayers and your devotion to Christ leading the way.

16

Facing Failure

> Let us therefore come boldly to the throne of grace, that we may obtain mercy and find grace to help in time of need.
>
> *Hebrews 4:16*

In our early lives, we are full of hope and ambitions. We can't wait to meet that special someone with whom we will fall in love, marry, and live with for the rest of our lives. We all want to belong to someone, to be special to someone. But how do we get past the devestating blow that tells us we aren't as special as we thought?

One of the hardest realities I had to face in my divorce was my helplessness in changing my husband's mind, my utter inability to control his decisions. Standing hopelessly by and watching a good man and devoted father change before my eyes was a desperate feeling. Realizing my dream was vanishing was unbearable.

There is no other place to take our failure than the heart of Jesus. Hear these words. "I can do all things through Christ who strengthens me" (Phil. 4:13).

March boldly to His throne, bow before Him, and receive the deep cup of grace He has for you. Even a sense of failure is no match for that kind of strength.

Resurrection power is available for you today, and it's the only power that will help.

17

If Only I Had ...

If we confess our sins, He is faithful and just to forgive us our sins and to cleanse us from all unrighteousness.

1 John 1:9

The "If Only" disease can kill you! *If only I had tried harder, if only I had been prettier, if only I weren't so fat, if only, if only, if only.* . . . The list goes on and on.

There is not one of us, married or divorced, who measures a perfect one hundred on the ruler of perfect living. We all make mistakes. We all bite our tongues and wish with all our hearts that we could go back in time and change a decision, undo a hurtful word, live our lives a little differently.

What do we do with the "if onlys" in our lives? We make a conscious decision to let them go or else we can never move on in victory.

Your "if only" is no better or no worse than the next person's. Maybe you've made a list of sins, from bad to not-so-bad, and you've decided yours must be the worst. Wrong. Sin is sin. One woman may be unfaithful to her mate. That's sin. Another woman may be faithful, but mentally cruel. That's sin, too. God doesn't rate sin on a scale of one to ten.

Go to Him with all your "if onlys," from the least to the biggest. Know that when the nails cracked the bones in His palms, and the first drop of blood began to fall, all of your "if onlys" were covered. Believe it.

18

VICTIMS

For He has not despised nor abhored the affliction of the afflicted; nor has He hidden His face from Him; but when He cried to Him, He heard.
Psalm 22:24

Who was the victim in your divorce? Most likely, you're screaming a loud "me"!

Recently, I watched the home video of *Gone with the Wind,* and I was struck anew with the tragic figure of Rhett Butler. He loved Scarlett and was willing to hand her anything. Yet there was no way he could control her emotions and make her love him back. I turned off the TV and thought, *Rhett Butler was the most tragic victim in this movie!*

Then I thought about Scarlett. Her selfishness and manipulative antics kept her from ever being able to truly love anyone. *Perhaps,* I thought, *Scarlett was the most tragic victim in this movie, after all.* Excessive love of self is surely the victim's prison.

Is it possible that there was more than one victim in your divorce? You may have received the hardest blows, cried the loudest, and hurt the most, but the other party may be a victim of inescapable habits, torturous addictions, selfish ambitions, and blinding self-love.

Who is the victim in divorce? The answer is everyone involved.

19

Who Won Anyway?

> Yet in all these things we are more than conquerors through Him who loved us.
> *Romans 8:37*

When the court trial was all over, the papers signed, and the finances settled, who actually won? Maybe you came out with financial security, you're glad your former spouse "got what he or she deserved," and you feel you've won. Or perhaps all you saved is gone, your dignity destroyed, your self-esteem ripped apart, and you know you've lost. Perhaps he or she became custodial parent. You feel that you've lost because you can only see your children in limited visits. And maybe you're so glad to be free that you don't even care who won.

The truth is that when a marriage ends in divorce no one wins and everyone loses. Oh, you might win the temporary battle, be released from daily pain, and sleep easier at night. You may be free from the binding insecurities and fear in your home. But you lose something else.

You lose a little of yourself. Your children lose a connected family, your in-laws lose a member of their family, your close friends lose a couple they loved, and you lose a sense of your ability to succeed.

But even though you lose at divorce, you don't have to be a loser. You can win while losing. You can even be a conqueror—more than a conqueror because of Jesus.

20

Can't We Just Skip Forgiveness?

> "For if you forgive men their trespasses, your heavenly Father will also forgive you. But if you do not forgive men their trespasses, neither will your Father forgive your trespasses."
> *Matthew 6:14–15*

Maybe you have an attitude like that of a member of one of my divorce support groups. When I announced that the topic discussed at the next session would be forgiveness, the woman said, "Oh, B.J. Can't we just skip that? Let's wait until my court trial is over, and I've gotten my fair share. Then I'll deal with forgiveness!"

While I appreciate her honest reply, to the Christian, forgiveness is a command, not an option. But we must also remember that forgiveness doesn't mean that we are to become someone else's doormat. It doesn't mean that we are to cower under another's oppresive rule or sit back and take whatever abuse that is handed us.

Still, the words of Jesus ring true. If we want forgiveness, then we must also forgive. Forgiveness means freeing yourself from someone else's control. Forgiveness means erasing another's misconduct from your thoughts so that oppression doesn't keep you tied in knots. Forgiveness is a vital, necessary, continuing element in your healing process. Without forgiveness, you will never grow through—or heal from—your divorce.

Be honest with God. You can tell Him you'd rather skip this scriptural advice, but you know you can't. Tell Him you don't know how to forgive, but you know He does.

With His spirit at work in your heart, you will soon know the refreshing, releasing power that forgiveness brings. Trust Him with this task, just as you trust Him to forgive you.

21

GOD IS LISTENING

> "I have heard your prayer. I have seen your tears; surely I will heal you."
>
> *2 Kings 20:5*

This verse is a favorite among my divorce support groups. Its beautiful words always comfort the brokenhearted.

Isn't it wonderful to know that God is watching you this very moment? He is mindful of your pain. He has seen the tears streaming down your face. He wants you to know that He cares and that He plans to bring healing to your wounds.

You can take these words into your heart as a personal promise from God to you. He doesn't plan to leave you in your misery. He isn't going to turn away from you as you cry. No, He is watching you closely, aware that you are in pain, and He has plans for your recovery.

Your job is to trust Him to provide the solution rather than to try and provide for your own healing. You don't need to rush here and there seeking comfort in the wrong places or in the wrong company of people.

God has something better for you. His healing plan will be complete and beautiful. He will begin showing it to you very soon.

Write this comforting verse on an index card. But to begin the verse, write "Dear [and please write *your name here*]." And end the verse by signing it, "Love, your Father."

Accept that this promise is for you, and soon you will know His personal plan for your healing.

22

ONE WOMAN'S TURNING POINT

But thanks be to God, who gives us the victory through our Lord Jesus Christ.
1 Corinthians 15:57

A newly divorced woman called me often on the phone. Her pain was still fresh; the shock, so devestating. She needed to talk, and over and over again she recounted the events of her divorce. Married over twenty-five years, she and her husband were pillars of their church. Suddenly he was gone, leaving an emptiness that seemed overwhelming.

She continually cried. Repeatedly, her voice echoed her shame and bitterness. "How could he," she asked, "do this to me?"

After many months of calling and crying, her voice suddenly took a note of optimism. With the first hint of hope I had heard, she said, "I've decided I've got to stop concentrating on what I don't have and begin thinking about what I do have!"

Wise words. Healing words. Overcoming words. Victory words. Turning point words. She began to go upward from that day on.

Thanks be to God who gives the victory through Jesus!

23

Letting Go

> The simpleton believes every word he hears, but the prudent man looks and considers well where he is going. A wise man suspects danger and cautiously avoids evil, but the fool bears himself insolently and is presumptuously confident.
>
> *Proverbs 14:15, AMP*

She sat crying week after week, caught in a trap of her choosing. Her ex-husband was with another woman, yet he called regularly to keep her on his hook.

He called to check on her. He called to hint there might be another chance for them. He called to unload his guilt. Someone in our divorce support group said, "Don't answer the phone." Another said, "Hang up on him." But she still loved him. She could not give up the hope that maybe—just maybe—he would come back, even though month after month his lifestyle continued.

Somewhere I learned this statement: a man convinced against his will is of the same opinion still.

There was no way we could convince her against her will. She had to learn through years of lost dreams that he was not coming home. He probably had never even entertained the thought.

Read these verses carefully. Ask God to guard you against a simple mind that lacks wisdom. Ask Him to lead you to the truth.

You are worth much more than to be someone else's convenience. Any man (or woman) openly having an affair—while telling you he or she might come back—is a clever manipulator. That's not love. That's cruelty. Ask God to help you to let go.

24

TAKE TIME TO HEAL

> To everything there is a season, a time for every purpose under heaven: a time to be born, and a time to die; a time to plant, and a time to pluck what is planted; a time to kill, and a time to heal; a time to break down, and a time to build up.
>
> *Ecclesiastes 3:1–3*

This is your season to heal. Take time for it. Let the season do its complete work in you.

I've heard various counselors say that we need to give ourselves one-and-a-half to three years to heal the wounds of divorce. I always tell my support groups that this doesn't mean one-and-a-half to three years of never-ending pain. It means a period of time in which you must be patient with yourself while you heal. There will be moments of laughter and fun during this season; but for healing to do its proper work, you and I must realize that healing takes time.

But time doesn't heal. Jesus heals. He uses time if we turn the hours of each day over to Him.

You will have friends and relatives who want to speed up your season of grief. Unless someone has walked the walk you are now walking, they might be impatient with your wounds.

That's okay. Thank them for their concern, love them, and then move on with your own healing work. In the end, only you and God need to be pleased with the results.

25

A Different Love

> But I say to you, love your enemies, bless those who curse you, do good to those who hate you, and pray for those who spitefully use you and persecute you.
>
> *Matthew 5:44*

People going through divorce often have a difficult time separating love from need. After living a while with their spouse, they aren't sure if the pain is because they love that person or because they're just used to the person being around. We grow dependent on one another. Now the question begins to swirl around in our thoughts, *What is love, anyway?*

When my husband left me, I grieved because I could no longer share hugs, hear his laughter, or enjoy watching him with our sons.

But I quickly learned that love has another side. I learned I didn't have to stop loving him. I just had to learn to love in a different way. I learned to love him from a distance. That meant that while I couldn't be involved in his life, I could continue caring about him as a human being.

This kind of love, *agape* love, is a love that expects nothing in return. You might not think you can ever love your ex-husband (or ex-wife) again.

By yourself, you can't. This kind of miracle only occurs as Jesus brings forth His healing in you.

26

WHAT'S WRONG WITH ME?

In the multitude of my anxious thoughts within me, your comforts cheer and delight my soul!
Psalm 94:19, AMP

A divorced person described the humiliation well: "I feel I have a huge *D* marked on my forehead. I'm branded for life!"

After a divorce it's easy to become paranoid when we consider our circumstances. We often imagine that others are talking about us. We feel sure that the church we attend views us differently, and that our neighbors think something must be terribly wrong with us.

I found that watching other happy couples was especially painful at first. *They* could keep their marriage together. Why couldn't I?

But it takes two who are commited, who can trust, and who want things to work out. But don't be too hard on yourself. Moving you to victory is one of God's specialties. Let His grace gently pull that *D* from your forehead and His comfort cheer and delight your soul!

27

SEARCHING FOR HOPE

Why are you cast down, O my soul? And why are you disquieted within me? Hope in God, for I shall yet praise Him for the help of His countenance.

Psalm 42:5

We look for hope everywhere. We search the faces of family and friends. We seek its promise in the voices of television comedians. We watch others, desperately trying to assure ourselves that hope still exists.

But friends often don't know what to say. Family members are often too upset—their grief closely tied to our own. Others glibly tell us that everything will be okay, and comedians only make us laugh for a few minutes. Soon reality returns, and hope seems to be on a faraway planet. No one can give you hope.

Our only hope comes, as the psalmist says, in God. *Hope in God.* In your exasperating search, only He can quietly and gently slip hope into your days.

You'll know when it happens. Suddenly the morning looks a little brighter than yesterday. You get dressed with a little more zest, and you notice—maybe for the first time in months—that the little pane in your window is bringing a bright ray of sun on your carpet.

Thank God for the gift of hope. Expect that it will come. Hope in God. He has a great big bundle saved up for you today.

28

Grieving

> Now may the God of patience and comfort grant you to be like-minded toward one another, according to Christ Jesus.
>
> *Romans 15:5*

Grief is all consuming. You can think of nothing but your own pain. It doesn't matter that there is a whole world out there with problems of its own. Yours matter the most. That's how I was. Then I met a lady down the street. A tragic accident had taken her husband's body and his mind. Now an invalid, he needed total care. She bathed him, moved him from the bed to the wheelchair, and sat for hours keeping him company while he only groaned and screamed.

In some strange way I silently joined my hands to hers, and everyday after that as I passed her home on the way to school, I thought, *Pain lives there, too. I'm not the only one who hurts.*

Of course that didn't make my hurt go away. But it did give me a sister. And when I wept for her, my consuming grief jumped in the back seat, if only for a moment.

Finally I could feel someone else's pain besides my own. Something inside of me loosened. Surely healing was on its way.

29

CAN I EVER TRUST AGAIN?

I said in my haste, all men are deceitful and liars.
Psalm 116:11, AMP

I made a statement I truly believed: "I will never trust another man again!"

During that period I decided all men must be alike. There never would be one I could trust. Besides, why should I ever again allow myself to be in the vulnerable position of being hurt? I felt safer this way.

Years later, after being a part of many divorce support groups, I learned that many divorced men feel the same way about women. Men and women may look different on the outside, but inside they're bundles of need when an unwanted divorce lands at their door. We both hurt the same. We cry the same. Our self-esteem plummets to an all-time low. We're afraid to love again.

Fortunately, the statement I made eventually melted away. I learned that I couldn't judge the whole male population by the acts of one man. To live again, I had to learn to trust again.

Cautiously, hesitantly, like a child learning to walk, I began to heal. I leaned on the arm of the only Man I knew I could trust for sure—Jesus. With His steady grip leading the way, I moved out once again into life.

30

Is God Mad at Me?

For the Lord, the God of Israel, says: I hate divorce and marital separation.
Malachi 2:16, AMP

Once I asked my divorce support group if any of them thought God was mad at them. One responded, "I do wonder sometimes what He has against me."

Let me assure you. God is not out to get you. He is not the author of your divorce. Read the above verse to know exactly what God thinks of divorce. He hates divorce because He knows the hurt that will result. He hates divorce because it is completely contrary to all He is and stands for. Divorce divides; God unites. Divorce brings strife; God gives peace.

But He knows that, just as disease is a part of our fallen world, so is discontent and brokenness. God may hate divorce, but He doesn't hate you because you are divorced.

God is love and God loves me. Say those words over and over and rest in the certainty that a God who represents love is not out to get you.

31

BECOMING REAL

Lord, my heart is not haughty, nor my eyes lofty; neither do I exercise myself in matters too great or in things too wonderful for me. Surely I have calmed and quieted my soul, like a weaned child with his mother; like a weaned child is my soul within me.

Psalm 131:1–2, AMP

It's encouraging to see separated and divorced people learn one of life's hardest but greatest lessons: no one is self-sufficient. All need a Savior.

It's encouraging to see a person begin the exciting journey of becoming real. It doesn't happen overnight, but if you'll let divorce work *for* you instead of against you, you will arrive at your destination a new, whole, and beautiful person. Many of my group members tell me they actually like themselves better now than before their divorce.

Divorce can have a truly liberating effect on those who are truly commited to growth. Before their divorce, it may have been their goal to be seen by others as being a perfect family, as perfect mates and perfect parents.

Divorce chisels away our masks and our pride, making us take a good look at who we really are. Divorce—when turned over to Jesus for growth—can even have a softening effect.

David wrote the psalm used to begin this devotion on becoming real—David the mighty warrior, David the king, David whose pride caused him to commit adultery and plan a murder. At the time he wrote this psalm, he was a broken man. But in his brokenness, he had become real, loveable, and much more aware of humanity.

Take Jesus' hand. Walk with Him by your side as you begin the journey of becoming real. You'll never look back.

EPILOGUE

Moving on with Life

When the first shock of pain entered my crumbling marriage, I knew of no close friends or family who had experienced what I was having to face. I remember thinking, *If I could just meet someone who has felt my pain and is still alive to tell about it—even able to smile again—I could have some hope.*

But one day, the healing began and then continued in my life. At that point, I made a decision: Maybe I could be that somebody for the others who were just starting out on this journey! After all, I had learned to smile again. Perhaps I could reach out and help someone else.

With this in mind, I made an announcement at a Christian single's gathering: "I'm having a spaghetti dinner at my home on January 21st. Everyone separated or divorced is welcomed to attend." I told them the time and how to get to my home. Then I solicited help in making preparations.

My mother and a neighbor made spaghetti, and others pitched in with the seating arrangements and table decorations. We filled my unfurnished living room with tables from the church and placed white tablecloths and candles on each table. Then I sat back and waited. Would anybody come?

Twenty-two people arrived. I knew only a couple of them. We had a glorious evening together. Throughout the meal I heard comments such as "It's been so long since I've been to a candlelight dinner!"

I was hooked. I fell in love with these new friends. The spaghetti dinner launched the beginning of our first divorce support groups, which were held monthly on Sunday afternoons at the Methodist church I attended. Sometimes guest speakers came; other times we had panel discussions with some of our members. My mother became the self-appointed refreshment committee. Always, the spirit was happy as we bonded through our mutual need.

Sunday afternoons were only a part of our fellowship, however. My home now became an open door for separated and divorced men and women. As soon as I got home from my job teaching first grade, the phone or doorbell began ringing.

We drank many cups of coffee, shed many tears, and had many prayers around my kitchen table. People were even coming from towns within a fifty-mile radius. Before I knew it, over one hundred people were in our group.

The experience was consuming, but thrilling. I realized God had placed a ministry in my lap. How I loved this work and those coming to my home! They quickly won my heart.

In the twelve years I have been having groups, I have learned a few things. The first group was so large that individual ministry was difficult. Divorced people are not always able to keep their commitments, due to unforseen struggles that pop up from time to time. Our Sunday afternoon meetings usually had a few regular folks, but the turnover was tremendous. Keeping up with the faithful and the stragglers was almost overwhelming.

Now, I have smaller groups of three to seven people. We meet one night a week for eight weeks, either in a church or in the home of one of the members. Once I was asked by a school counselor to have a support group for parents, and we met once a week at night in the school conference room. Lately, I've had groups in my home. I prefer a home environment because we can be informal and cozy.

I always give my philosophy before someone agrees to come. First, our group is dependent on God for healing. We realize that He is our ultimate source. Second, our time together is a commitment. Members are expected to always be present unless there is sickness or some prearranged commitment. Third, we will start promptly and end two hours later, with a refreshment break in between.

When I lay out the guidelines, the members always respond well and take this period of growth seriously. I remind them that eight weeks will not cure all their needs, but if they will work at it, this time together will be a vital part of their healing process.

At our first meeting together, I tell them my story and why I have divorce support groups. I also make very sure they know that I am not a counselor. I'm just somebody who has been through it and is still alive to tell about it! Our groups are informal and loving. We hug each other. We cry together, and we reach out to help.

As each group ends, I feel that part of my heart is leaving. I rejoice with them later when new loves walk into their lives, and I'm honored to be invited to their weddings. Recently, two members in different groups met and married. I was honored to be asked to write a poem for them and to read it at their wedding. I titled it "Second Chance," and I will never forget the joy of that day.

On one occasion, I watched a beautiful woman sit on my sofa for eight weeks while a charming man viewed her with much respect from across the room. I saw a relationship brewing, but he was too much of a gentleman to break the bond of our group by asking her out. At the end of the eight weeks, they began dating and later married.

I have had several groups bond so well that they continue meeting after I go to form another group.

One such group met for two years and became best friends in the process.

God has blessed me so much by allowing me the privilege of working with divorced people. I love to show them that there is hope. I love to show them that there is life after divorce. With each new group, I grow a little more in my own healing. With each new group, I am reminded of how important God's hurting people are. And with each new group, I gain valuable friendships.

God has also blessed my life with a new relationship with a godly man I love dearly and who loves me. At the time of my divorce, I never dreamed I would be so blessed again. But whether I (or you) remain single or remarry, I know the most important thing in life is to keep God first and follow His loving guidance. For He knows the best plans for us all.

> For I know the thoughts and plans that I have for you, says the Lord, thoughts and plans for welfare and peace, and not for evil, to give you hope in your final outcome.
> *Jeremiah 29:11*, AMP